T0079882

HOW TO WOO,

WHEN, AND TO WHOM.

HOW TO WOO,

WHEN, AND TO WHOM.

"Cela est plaisant, oui, ce mot de marriage,
il n'est rien de plus drôle pour les jeunes filles.
Ah! Nature! Nature!"—MOLIERE

First published in 2006 by the Bodleian Library
Broad Street, Oxford, OX1 3BG

www.bodleianbookshop.co.uk

ISBN 1 85124 345 3
ISBN 13 978 1 85124 345 7

Designed by Melanie Gradtke
Printed and bound by L.E.G.O. S.p.A., Vicenza, Italy
British Library Catalogue in Publishing
A CIP record of this publication is available from the British Library

Reproduced from *How to Woo, When, and to Whom* (London, Ward & Lock,
1855), Bodleian Library, 24731 e.33 (10).

INTRODUCTION

The desire to be married, which most young people indulge in vehemently, is no new passion; nor is it, nor will it be, confined to our present age. If people wonder why in certain very reputable journals they see many matrimonial advertisements, or why a "Matrimonial Agency" exists, their astonishment may perhaps be abated when they are told that, almost as soon as newspapers were established, such methods of matrimonial alliance were adopted; and that in a very early one may be found a paragraph stating, that "A young woman is willing to alter her condition, provided she can find a worthy, honest man, who must be one of those despised people called Methodists." Indeed, the words and terms are almost the same as would be used to-day by a very serious young person; so that the charge of our present young ladies not being so retiring as their grandmothers falls to the ground.

Matrimony, which is the first institution in the world, is also one of the most important. To the majority of the people of any country it matters little whether they be well governed, but it is all-important that they be well married. What king or governor may sit on the throne, the working man little cares about, but what sort of a woman sits at the head of his table is, to him, all-important.

Too much, therefore, cannot be attached to the choice of a wife; nor can any one be too careful in the guidance of his or her passions and wishes; for these last, whatever the fantastical poets may say, are more the subjects of control than most people are willing to own. Upon one side, as in the old fable of the choice of Hercules between virtue and vice, stand certain misery, bickerings, discontent, and an inaptitude either for business or enjoyment; on the other, calm feelings, happiness, and domestic pleasure, and thence arising a fitness both for this world and the next.

Such "a consummation, most devoutly", indeed, "to be wished", depends upon the first step taken by the parties engaged. The *choice*, the *time*, and the *manner*, are each important subjects of consideration and advice; and it is upon these that this little book seeks *to advise*. Its contents will be digested in the manner of maxims, as by that means much will be comprehend in the fewest words, as space is valuable.

The writer may add, that by a kind of necessity the order of the subjects has been different; and, as the reader will perceive, stands thus:— "When to woo, to whom, and how." Under the latter head it has, in this short treatise, not been thought advisable to give any specimens of that correspondence termed "Love-letters."

WHEN TO WOO.

AGE AND WORLDLY AFFAIRS.

Both men and women vary greatly as to the age at which they arrive at maturity; marriage should never be undertaken before that age, and generally *never* after.

Age is to be counted from two qualities—the health of the subject, and the formation of his or her character.

In uncertain health marriage should not be ventured upon. Presupposing affection, without which matrimony can scarcely be holy, to dower either wife or husband with ill-health is cruel; to chance a speedy separation by death, ridiculous and wicked.

An early formation of character, when accompanied by an equal growth and strength of body, may be taken as equivalent to age; for it is character and knowledge which make age.

> "It may be the *calendar of years*
> Your are the elder man, *but 'tis the sun*
> *Of knowledge* on the mind's dial
>   shining bright,
> And chronicling thoughts and deeds,
> That makes true time."

Should the character of the future partner in life be already formed, and, being firmly established, be diametrically opposed to your own, any thoughts of union would be madness.

A similarity of disposition in wife and husband should be sought for. The pleasures of the one should be reflected in the mind of the other.

Worldly circumstances need not be very excellent, or sufficient for superfluity, let it suffice if they be enough for competence; but at the time of marriage they should present a reasonable probability of increase, or, at the least, of a firm certainty.

That the foregoing is based upon truth, and that it is widely acted upon, is proved by the Registrar-General's returns, wherein we find that directly the country becomes prosperous marriages increase.

When you are sure that you love a certain person deeply, and that that person loves you, marry if possible. More misery has been occasioned by delay, neglect, or marriages for money, than by those which at the first might be termed imprudent.

Whatever the talk of the world is, it by no means follows that a young man's progress in life is stopped by marriage; on the contrary, with the great majority, the intellects become sharpened, the morals improved, and the energy, by a certain necessity, enlarged. It requires but little wisdom to see that these three qualities form the main-spring of progress and advancement in the world.

Lord Bacon says, in his Essays, that "A wife and children are impediments to great enterprises, either of virtue or mischief." Lord Bacon very seldom said anything more false. He could easily have been confuted by examples of his own time, or before him. To do so now we are only troubled by an *embarass de richesses*. Shakespere, Milton, and Cromwell were married men. Indeed, with but few exceptions, all our best poets, divines, and lawgivers were so also; and, to completely confute so unguarded a statement, it needs us but to look around, and to observe that those nations which possess the most energy— the Americans, English, French, and Swiss—are those which are also most given to marriage.

No union should be undertaken until both of the contracting parties are fully acquainted with each other's dispositions.

It has been said, and can scarcely be too frequently repeated, that "When desire or passion is based upon love, the marriage will prove a happy one, and the love prove lasting; when love arises from desire, it is but fictitious, and will but ensure misery."

If either man or woman are subject to indulge in any foible, or known vice, such as irritability, idleness, love of scandal, drunkenness, or worse, he or she should not marry till that vice is conquered.

When a man finds that he is more easily attracted by male than female society—that the presence of children is irksome—that the cares, and duties, and responsibilities which marriage entails will be too heavy for him—he should not indulge in any idea of marriage.

When a woman knows a man to be addicted to any known self-indulgence, or to that which the world too frequently calls pleasure, she should discountenance him.

When before union there is an unreasonable, absurd, and romantic degree of affection, that marriage will probably be an unhappy one. There is some truth in Boswell's epigram upon the subject:—

"Whilst courting, and in honey-moon,
    With Kate's allurements smitten,
I loved her late, I loved her soon,
    And called her dearest kitten;
But now my kitten's grown a cat,
    And cross, like other wives,
Alas! alas! my honest Mat,
    I fear she has nine lives."

Dr. Johnson has somewhere said, that the better husband a man makes, the better citizen and better man he is. When a man is convinced of the truth of that maxim he should marry.

Late marriages, that is, those undertaken when people are advanced in life, are more frequently productive of unhappiness than early matches. The reason is, that not only are the husband and wife physically more unfitted to each other, but also their peculiarities are more strongly marked, and their characters are more formed, so that they do not bend to each other's will, or consult each other's tastes, so much as younger people.

To sum up: People should marry—when of age sufficient to be stable, not stubborn—when their circumstances or fortunes are easy, and have a reasonable hope of increase—when they meet with one whose tastes, whose religion, whose morals, and whose habits of thinking they admire—when their love is firm and ardent, but at the same time reasonable—when they themselves are capable of making many little sacrifices, and, in return for much comfort and enjoyment, they can themselves afford to the object of their love many kindnesses, much condescension, and much time—and, lastly, when they are perfectly sure that their love is built upon reason, not upon caprice.

Our last maxim upon this head shall be from one who said many wise things, but nothing wiser than this:—

"When that you are going to marry, do not expect more from life than life will afford. You may often find yourself out of humour, and you may often think your wife not studious enough to please you; and yet you may have reason to consider yourself, upon the whole, very happily married."

TO WHOM.

The want of judgement is the cause of all ill-sorted marriages, and through them of a great part of the misery of this world.

As people are taught where to go on the ice, by notices which tell them where they should not go, so, perhaps, they may be taught whom to marry by an express warning whom not to marry.

In fitness for matrimonial obligation, several things are to be considered:—Age, health, temper, fortune, morals, position in society, acquirements, individualities.

As to age, it is generally conceded that the wife should be younger than the husband. In regard to this, Shakespere gives a reason which is by no means flattering to the superior sex:—

"————Let still the woman take
An elder than herself; so wears she to him,
So sways the level in her husband's heart.
For, boy, however we do praise ourselves,
Our fancies are more giddy and infirm,
More longing, wavering, sooner lost and won,
Than women's are."

It is however, to be remarked that the first love of
men of genius is frequently bestowed upon women
elder than themselves. Possibly they are attracted
by their staid demeanour and their sense, and share
in Hazlitt's antipathy "to giggling girls."

Health should be made an especial consideration;
as we have before said, neither the sick nor the infirm
are proper subjects for marriage. When both man and
woman are weakly, matters are rendered worse.

Our next maxim embraces morals, fortune, and
temper; and upon it we cannot do better than quote

the words of the wise and able Cecil, Lord Burghleigh,
a man who knew not less how to govern his own estate
than the kingdom of his royal mistress:—

THE CHOICE OF A WIFE.— "When it shall please
God to bring thee to man's estate, use great provi-
dence and circumspection in choosing thy wife, *for
from thence will spring all thy future good or evil.* And
it is an action of life, like unto a stratagem of war,
wherein a man can err but once. If thy estate be good,
match near home and at leisure; if weak, far off and
quickly. Enquire diligently her disposition, and how
her parents have been inclined (descended) in their
youth. Let her not be poor, how generous (well born)
soever; for a man can buy nothing in the market with
gentility; nor choose a base and uncomely creature
altogether for wealth, for it will cause contempt in
others and loathings in thee. Neither make choice
of a dwarf nor a fool; for by the one thou shall beget
a race of pigmies, the other will be thy continual

disgrace; and it will *yirke* thee to hear her talk; for thou shall find it, to thy great grief, that there is nothing more fulsome than a she-fool."

From the above the reader should subtract that policy which was the fashion of the times, and would now be counted duplicity, and he will find it then adapted to the present and indeed to every age.

Position in society is frequently reckoned as more than equivalent for riches. Yet neither a wise man nor woman will seek to marry greatly out of their sphere of life; for if their partner be from a rank above them, their pride will frequently be wounded, and they will suffer from patronage; if from below their state in society, they will be annoyed in another, but no less acute, manner, and will find that no critics in the world are more ill-natured than those relations who are below them in wealth or in worldly position.

For aquirements look more to solid knowledge, either in wife or husband, than to accomplishments.

A learned wife is not to be shunned. Dr. Johnson has maintained that a woman would not be the worse wife for being learned; but it is a question whether the wife should be more learned than the husband. In a poem by Sir Thomas Overbury, we find the following:—

> "Give me next good—an understanding wife;
>   By nature wise, not learned by much art;
> Some knowledge on her side will, all my life,
>   More scope of conversation impart,
> Besides her inborne virtue fortify.—
> They are most good who best know why."

By individualities we are to understand qualities natural and peculiar to certain people. Phrenologists balance the preponderance of one organ by the activity of another. Thus too great *acquisitiveness* would result in dishonesty if not balanced by *conscientiousness*. Therefore if the person whom you seek to marry be very irritable, that quality may be amended by a forgiving disposition, and is to be looked over; but secret, suspicious, ungenerous, and mean natures are by all means to be avoided as partners for life.

The doctrine that "reformed rakes make the best husbands," and that "young men must sow their wild oats," are but mere excuses for immorality—and bad excuses too. The very best authority tells us, "that as men sow they will reap," and experience assures us that nothing is so difficult to efface as the early traces of vice. Young ladies are earnestly warned against indulging in such hopes.

Never marry those who merely possess beauty. "If," says Lady Mary Wortley Montagu, "I had all the personal charms that I want, a face is too slight a foundation for happiness. You would be soon tired with seeing every day the same thing." And again, "If we marry," she is writing to her future husband;

"if we marry, our happiness must consist in loving one another; 'tis principally my concern to think of the most probable method of making that love eternal."

To sum up:— Those whom to marry are those most fitted to ourselves; to whom our tastes will be appreciated; those who have fixed principles of religion and virtue; those who are healthy in body and sound in mind; those who in complexion and in spirit are most opposite to ourselves; those whom we can honour and esteem; those who have hitherto led a pure and blameless life; and those to whom you are ardently attached, so that your felicity may not be the matter of a month but of a life.

HOW.

Young ladies, and with reason, naturally object, on so important an occasion, to be the last to be consulted. Consequently, the gentleman should first make sure that the affections of the young lady would, *in all probability*, centre upon himself, before he proposes to the parents or guardians.

Marriage is so *personal* a business, that it will be readily conceded that it concerns the contracting parties more than it does relations and friends. For this reason the maxim above should always be acted upon.

A man of honour will ascertain that his attentions are agreeable to a lady without entrapping the affections of the lady herself; which course would, should the engagement from family reasons fall to the ground, entail certain misery upon her.

As for the ladies, a writer in the *New Quarterly Review* says, that *"No man of sense doubts for an instant but that any woman can marry any man she chooses."* Such being conceded, it is almost superfluous to lay down any rules for their method of proceeding, that being best known to themselves.

The foregoing, like all truths, has its exceptions; but given time, opportunity, and place, it is doubtlessly perfectly true.

If it be unnecessary to lay down rules of action for ladies, it is yet so to remind them of their art; and to assure the unskilful that forwardness, flirting, and expressive speeches form no part of it.

Shakespere, whose wisdom is pre-eminent in everything, has not left this subject untouched. He has shown us the qualities which in a woman attract good men—and such only are worth attracting:—

> "A maiden, *never bold*
> Of spirit, so still and quiet, that her nature
> Blushed at herself."

And when such a maiden falls in love, he has taught us how she attracts to herself the heart of him she loves:—

> "These things to hear
> Would Desdemona seriously incline;
> *But still the house affairs would draw her*
> *   thence,*
> *Which, ever as she could with haste*
> *   despatch,*
>
> *She'd come again,* and with a greedy ear
> Devour up my discourse."

When by these means Desdemona has assured Othello of her preference, she takes another opportunity, but one perfectly consistent with the utmost modesty, to indirectly declare her love:—

> "My story being done,
> She gave me for my pains a world of sighs:
> * * * * *
> 'Twas pitiful! 'twas wondrous pitiful!
> She wished she had not heard it,
>   yet she wished
> That heaven had made her such a man.
>   She thanked me,
> And bade me, *if I had a friend that loved me,*
> *I should but teach him how to tell my story,*
> And that would win her.
>   *Upon this hint I spake.*"

Time and attention are frequently more valued, both by men and women, than presents or fervency of expression. "A man may give many presents," wrote on who knew her sex well, "because he is liberal and generous; or he may be ardent in his love because he is of a sanguine disposition; but if he devotes to me his *time,* I am sure that he loves me."

Nevertheless, presents are not in all cases to be neglected:—

> "Win her with gifts if she neglect thy words;
> Dumb jewels often, in their silent kind,
> More than rich words do move a
>   woman's mind."

Love-letters are often very absurd things when (as they sometimes are) made public. The reason is, they concern only two people in the world—the writer and the receiver. They should be plain, fervent, respectful, and to the point. Never write a letter merely for the sake of writing; let it always have some aim—a message, an invitation; or let it carry news of some kind.

Before acceptance, the young lady should be addressed as "Dear Madam;" after acceptance, the Christian name may be used.

If people let the heart speak, using care also to preserve common sense in their epistles, a love-letter will be perfectly correct, and as it should be—that is, earnest without being silly.

In case of rejection, the gentleman should at once, unless under peculiar circumstances, abstain from his suit. Unless he does so, his conduct becomes persecuting.

Ladies should never, by the slightest familiarity, encourage any one whom they would object to marry.

Rejection should be courteous, definite, and decisive; but couched in a manner that, whilst it deprives the suitor of hope, it inflicts no pain.

Engaged people should avoid compliments in company.

A proposal being made, the lady should first signify her own willingness, and then refer her suitor to her parents.

In public or in company the conduct of lovers should be guarded. Avoid all show of extreme preference. Neither caress nor chide before others.

Letters, trinkets, and presents, when engagements are broken off, are always returned by both parties.

Long engagements are dangerous. If a gentleman does not intend to marry a lady, he has no right to make his attentions peculiar. He should consider her true interest, and he would not trifle with her affections.

City Press, No. 1, Long Lane: W.H. Collingridge.